EARTHQUAKE SURVIVAL GUIDE

Linda Bohm

Published by Linda Bohm

Copyright 2015 Linda Bohm

Other Titles by Linda Bohm

Rapture Survival Guide

License Notes

Cover Photo Attribution

Earthquake Survival Guide

What is an earthquake?

When you hear the word earthquake, most people think of California, but earthquakes can occur anywhere on the earth. Earthquakes occur every day all over the earth, but most of them are too small for most people to feel. The degree that you feel the quake depends on how close you are to the epicenter, the point where the earthquake originated, and how large the quake is. The closer you are to the epicenter, the more damage that will occur depending on the size of the earthquake. The larger the earthquake, the greater the amount of damage that will occur.

An earthquake is caused when a fault line or plate boundary ruptures or shifts. The crust of the earth is made up of tectonic plates that lie next to each other. The boundary where the plates meet is where the most earthquakes occur. There are three types of plate boundaries; convergent, divergent and transform. A convergent boundary occurs when the plate either forms a subduction zone, where one plate slides beneath the other, or causes a plate collision. A divergent boundary occurs when the two plates slide apart from each other, this usually occurs under the ocean and this forms a new ocean floor. A transform boundary occurs when two plates grind past each other, the edges of the plates are jagged and as they grind against each other they can lock, while locked the stress builds up in the plates. Once the plates snap free and earthquake occurs. The most famous transform boundary is the San Andreas fault in California, the west side of the fault is moving north at 6 cm per year. Transform boundaries cause a lot of earthquakes.

That does not mean that there are no danger zones for earthquakes anywhere else. Intraplate earthquakes are areas that are not on the plate boundaries, but occur within the plate. They are rarer and are located at points where there is a weakness in the crust. One of the largest intraplate earthquakes occurred on the New Madrid fault line that runs through the central United States, it runs through Missouri, Arkansas, Tennessee, Kentucky, Illinois, Indiana and Mississippi. In 1811 and 1812 three strong earthquakes struck on this fault, it was one of the biggest earthquakes to hit the lower 48 states. The epicenter of the first earthquake was in New Madrid, Missouri on December 16th, 1811. At the time there were only about 500-600 people living in New Madrid. The ground began violently shaking, throwing people from their beds and overturning furniture. The quake was felt as far north as New York, Boston and Montreal, Canada and it rang church bells in Charleston, South Carolina. Seismic waves travel easily through bedrock which is what is under the Midwest and east coast. There were no seismographs to measure the quake but based on eyewitness accounts and the damage that was recorded the quake is estimated to be around 7.7 magnitude. Other effects of the earthquake were sulfur gas clouds that came up from the earth, and multiple aftershocks, some as big as the initial quake, sent buildings crashing to the ground, giant fissures opened in the ground, some swallowing homes. A large piece of land thrust up in the middle of the Mississippi river bed sending the water flowing backwards back upstream. Near the town of Little Prairie, the up thrust of the ground caused a nearby lake to disappear. Sand blows appeared all over the region from areas where the ground opened a small fissure and caused a water and sand mixture to shoot into the air.

After the earthquake was over and the aftershocks settled down, the people started rebuilding. On January 23, 1812 the second quake struck an estimated magnitude of 7.5. The same kinds of damage occurred as in the first earthquake and more aftershocks. Then on February 7, 1812 the last earthquake occurred, a magnitude 7.7. More sand blows, sulfuric clouds and collapsing riverbeds were only part of the effects. An area near the Mississippi river sunk down and the river rushed to fill it, creating a lake, Realfoot Lake, which still exists today.

Small earthquakes were triggered by these massive quakes, the Midwest experienced over 2,000 earthquakes and in the location of New Madrid, Missouri; 6,000-10,000 earthquakes were experienced; the activity lasted for five months. Before this earthquake no one thought that the area was seismically active, there had been no earthquakes in the area in recorded history. The loss of life is not known but it is estimated that it could be anywhere from 100-500 people. The only reason that there was not a large loss of life during these earthquakes is because it was sparsely populated at the time. If the same magnitude earthquakes would hit the area today the loss of life and property would be tremendous, thousands of people would be killed and the damage estimates would be in the billions. Bridges and highways would be destroyed, unreinforced brick and masonry buildings would collapse, river banks would collapse causing flooding, massive fissures would open causing sand blows and swallowing people, houses and cars, natural gas pipelines would break and fires would break out all over from fallen electrical wires and broken gas lines, water lines and blocked roads would make it difficult to put out fires. Before people can even recover from the damage there would be aftershocks and other earthquakes, some even larger than the initial quake. It would take years to recover from the earthquake and some places might never recover. According to a report created for FEMA and the U.S. Army Corp of Engineers by the Mid-America Earthquake Center at the University of Illinois, Institute for Crisis Disaster & Risk Management at George Washington University, the Central U.S. Earthquake Consortium, Innovative Emergency Management (IEM), and individual contributors the estimated loss of life for a 7.7 earthquake on the New Madrid fault line would be over 75,000 people and the cost would be $207 billion dollars.

Most earthquakes occur on the Pacific Ring of Fire. This is a 25,000 mile area in the Pacific basin where 75% of the world's active volcanoes are located, 90% of earthquakes occur on this ring. There are more than 450 volcanoes in the ring of fire and most of them are underneath the ocean. The edges of the ring of fire follow the plate boundaries in the Pacific basin. The ring runs up the west coast of North and South America, through the Aleutian trench, down off the coast of the island nations in Asia and then off the eastern coast of Australia and New Zealand and ending in Antarctica.

The largest earthquake that has been recorded is a 9.5 magnitude earthquake in Chile. The earthquake occurred on May 22, 1960 and lasted about 10 minutes. The epicenter was near Lumaco, about 350 miles south of Santiago. The city that was most affected by the earthquake was Valdivia. The earthquake triggered a tsunami that affected southern Chile, Hawaii, Japan, the Philippines, New Zealand, Australia and the Aleutian Islands. The Chilean coast had tsunamis up to 82 feet high, and 35 foot waves hit Hilo, Hawaii. The amount of casualties is not known but the estimate can be as high as 6,000 and the cost of $400-800 million dollars in 1960's figures (3.19 billion-6.38 billion today). The coastal tsunami completely wiped away many villages along the coast. The earthquake may have also set off the Cordon Caulle volcanic vent, which erupted. It is not known if other volcanoes also erupted due to lack of communication in the region. Landslides were triggered in the southern Andes Mountains but did not cause any fatalities because of low population in the area. Another landslide did block the Golgol River which caused it to burst out of an earthen dam creating a flood and destroying part of a road.

The largest American earthquake is a 9.2 magnitude earthquake that occurred on March 27, 1964. The epicenter was located 12 miles north of Prince William Sound, Alaska and 40 miles east of Anchorage, Alaska. This was the most powerful earthquake recorded in North American history and the third most powerful recorded by seismograph. It was also the third most powerful in recorded history. The earthquake triggered tsunamis that reached 220 feet high. The tsunami waves affected 20 countries reaching as far as Peru, New Zealand, Japan and Antarctica. The most damage was in Anchorage, Alaska, where much of the city was damaged by the quake and subsequent landslides. Most of the coastal towns in Prince William Sound, Kenai Peninsula and Kodiak Island were damaged by the earthquake, tsunamis and then fires that broke out. There were 139 casualties of this earthquake, 15 because of the quake, 106 from the tsunami in Alaska, 5 from the tsunami in Beverly Beach State Park, Oregon and 13 from the tsunami in Crescent City, California and the cost was $311 million ($2.28 billion in today's dollars).

What is an earthquake? Simply put, it is a violent shaking of the ground as a result of the movement of the earth's crust. The tectonic plates are constantly shifting; when they shift toward land they push the edge of the land inwards. When this occurs, the land that is being pushed inwards may slide under or over the fault line. At some point the friction will stop the sliding process and the land may be "stuck" for quite a while. Eventually the area will have too much pressure on it and the land will become unstuck, the energy released will cause waves through the crust, this results in an earthquake.

Largest World Earthquakes (Not Including the U.S.)			
Magnitude	Date	Location	
9.5	5/22/1960	Chile	
9.1	12/26/2004	Off the Coast of Sumatra, Indonesia	
9.0	3/11/2011	Honshu, Japan	
9.0	11/4/1952	Kamchatka	
8.8	2/27/2010	Off the Coast of Chile	
8.8	1/31/1906	Off the Coast of Ecuador	
8.6	3/28/2005	Northern Sumatra, Indonesia	
8.6	8/15/1950	Assam-Tibet	
8.6	4/11/2012	Off the Coast of Sumatra, Indonesia	
8.5	9/12/2007	Southern Sumatra, Indonesia	
8.5	2/3/1923	Kamchatka	
8.5	11/11/1922	Chile-Argentina Border	
8.5	10/13/1963	Kuril Islands	

Largest U.S. Earthquakes		
Magnitude	Date	Location
9.0	1/26/1700	Cascadia Subduction Zone
7.9	4/3/1868	Ka'u District, Island of Hawaii
7.9	1/9/1857	Fort Tejon, California
7.8	4/18/1906	San Francisco, California
7.8	2/24/1892	Imperial Valley, California
7.7	12/16/1811	New Madrid, Missouri
7.7	2/7/1812	New Madrid, Missouri
7.5	1/23/1812	New Madrid, Missouri
7.4	3/26/1872	Owens Valley, California
7.3	6/28/1992	Landers, California
7.3	8/18/1959	Hebgen Lake, Montana
7.3	7/21/1952	Kern County, California
7.3	1/31/1922	West of Eureka, California
7.3	9/1/1886	Charleston, South Carolina
7.3	11/23/1873	California and Oregon Coast
7.3	12/15/1872	North Cascades, Washington

Largest Alaskan Earthquakes		
Magnitude	Date	Location
9.2	3/28/1964	Prince William Sound, Alaska
8.7	2/4/1965	Rat Islands, Alaska
8.6	3/9/1957	Andreanof Islands, Alaska
8.2	11/10/1938	East of Shumagin Islands, Alaska
8.1	4/1/1946	Unimak Islands, Alaska
8.0	9/10/1899	Yakutat Bay, Alaska
7.9	11/3/2002	Denali Fault, Alaska
7.9	11/30/1987	Gulf of Alaska, Alaska
7.9	5/7/1986	Andreanof Islands, Alaska
7.9	9/4/1899	Near Cape Yakataga, Alaska
7.8	11/17/2003	Rat Islands, Alaska
7.8	2/10/1996	Andreanof Islands, Alaska

Types of Earthquakes

There are four different types of earthquake, and each occurs for different reasons. The four types are the tectonic earthquake, the volcanic earthquake, a collapse earthquake and an explosion earthquake.

The tectonic earthquake occurs when there is enough energy released on a fault line that causes the two sides of the fault to move against each other causing the earth to move. When the two faults move against each other it causes waves to radiate out from the epicenter and it releases the stored energy. This is the most common type of earthquake and the one that you think about when someone mentions the word earthquake. This can be the most widespread and the most widely felt quake type. The three other types are usually more specifically located and the damage is more localized. Depending on several factors such as the epicenter, the depth of the quake, the magnitude of the quake and the population density, these quakes can be minor or can be catastrophic. A tectonic earthquake can occur either on land or on the seabed, a quake on the ocean floor can even cause a tsunami warning. This kind of quake was seen in 2004 when a 9.1 magnitude earthquake, one of the largest ever recorded, off the coast of Sumatra struck on December 26th. The magnitude was so large that tsunamis were experienced in fourteen countries and devastated the coasts of Indonesia,

Sri Lanka, India and Thailand; At least 230,000 people lost their lives. This earthquake was so strong that it slightly changed the earth's rotation, and several some islands shifted south-west by anywhere from 8 inches to more than 4 feet. According to reports the energy released by this earthquake was similar to 26 megatons of TNT.

Tectonic earthquakes can be classified as either convergent, divergent or transform depending on the way that the plates move during the earthquake. A convergent boundary occurs when two tectonic plates move towards each other. When the oceanic plate, which is more dense, slides under the less dense plate, which can be continental or oceanic, this is called subduction. Because of these collisions earthquakes and volcanoes are common at this boundary. When a continental plate collides with another continental plate it may cause the plate to compress or subduct under the other plate; this has caused the creation of mountain ranges like the Himalayas. When two oceanic plates converge one will subduct under the other it creates an oceanic trench and an island arc or archipelago that is made up of a chain of volcanoes; like the Marian trench and the Mariana Islands. A divergent boundary occurs when two tectonic plates move away from each other. When this occurs on a continent it causes rift valleys, long and steep valleys formed by sinking land between plates. An example is the Rio Grande rift in New Mexico; this rift separates the Colorado Plateau in the west from the interior of the American continental plate. When this occurs on the sea bed, between oceanic plates, magma rises to fill in the gap. The magma does not usually rise above the gap between the tectonic plates, it rises to fill the gap and then hardens, the process then repeats. A rift valley is also created on the ocean floor, but it is more narrow than one on land and it runs along and oceanic ridge. A transform or slip strike fault is any type of fault that has a horizontal motion, where plates slide past each other. Unlike convergent and divergent faults there is no creation or destruction of the lithosphere, the outer shell of the planet. The most destructive transform faults are those on land at the borders of tectonic plates. The most famous transform boundary is the San Andreas Fault; the west side of the fault is slowly sliding north. Many earthquakes occur on the transform fault.

The volcanic earthquake is caused by the movement of magma. Magma is a basically liquefied rock that is ejected from a volcano. Since it is liquid, it is constantly moving even within the spaces between the rocks of a volcano. As the magma moves into or out of the spaces in the rocks there is a pressure change in the rock which may cause it to break and cause and earthquake. These are classified as volcano-tectonic earthquakes; these quakes do not mean that a volcanic eruption will occur. This kind of quake is similar to rain and moisture seeping into cracks in the ground that freezes in the winter, when spring comes the ice melts and the spaces it had occupied has now been weakened; the result will be the formation of a pothole. There is a second type of volcanic earthquake, a long period earthquake; these are caused by a steady movement of magma into the rocks. This type of earthquake will produce an eruption, the earthquakes will occur more frequently as the volcano gets ready to erupt. Scientists monitor all volcanoes so that they can be prepared for eruptions, seismographs are placed around the volcano to record any activity so that residents can be warned and evacuated in case of a probably eruption.

Collapse earthquakes are small earthquakes underground and in mines that are caused by the seismic waves produced by an explosion of rock on the surface. Many times this is caused by the roof of the mine collapsing. Mining causes weaknesses within the rock walls that make up the mine structure. When there are enough weaknesses within the structure that area may give way and cause an area of the mine to collapse. Some mines also use explosives to increase the size of the mines and open new tunnels, this also adds to the weakening of the mine structure. Once the walls are weakened it would not take too much to cause that area of the mine to collapse and to cause the roof to cave in. The seismic waves that are produced are similar to dropping a rock into the ocean. Waves spread out from the area that the stone was dropped; if the stone is large enough it could cause a tsunami. The waves spread out from the epicenter of the collapse and can cause further damage to other structures within the mine.

An Explosion earthquake is caused by the detonation of nuclear or chemical devices. When these devices are released underground the amount of pressure released causes an enormous release of energy that causes an earthquake. When countries test nuclear weapons the tests may be conducted underground. Testing the weapons underground lowers the amount of fallout from the radioactive debris. The earthquake magnitude that is triggered by these explosions depends on the amount of energy discharged by the weapon. These explosions create subsidence craters which are created when the surface of the area of the explosion collapses causing a sinkhole. The last underground nuclear test by the United States was in 1992, the Soviet Union, United Kingdom, China and France have also discontinued underground testing. Many countries have signed the Comprehensive Test Ban Treaty in 1996 which discontinued nuclear testing. The treaty has not been enforced because eight countries have not signed it including India, Pakistan and South Korea.

Magnitude and Waves

The severity of an earthquake is measured through the moment magnitude scale. This used to be called the Richter scale which was used from the 1930's through the 1970's, until it was replaced by the moment magnitude scale. The severity of the earthquake is measured by calculating the energy released during the quake. Magnitude is calculated logarithmically, so for each number you go up on the magnitude scale the amplitude (a measurement if the movement or vibration of something) of the ground movement goes up ten times. Based on this formula we can see that a magnitude 5 earthquake has ten times the ground shaking as a magnitude 4 earthquake and an 8.7 magnitude earthquake is 794 times bigger than a 5.8 magnitude earthquake. Magnitude also depends on the length of the fault, the longer the fault line the higher the magnitude that is possible.

Charles Richter developed the first method to determine the magnitude of an earthquake in 1934. The Richter scale was developed specifically for Southern California earthquakes, the calculations used were focused on the specific circumstances of the local earthquakes; this took into consideration the specific properties of the crust and mantle in the area. Richter used high frequency data from earthquakes to measure the intensity of the earthquake, up until magnitude 7 the results were fairly accurate. This was referred to as a local magnitude scale (ML). Other scales were developed to fill the gaps that the Richter scale could not cover including the body wave magnitude (Mb) and the surface wave magnitude (Ms). The body wave magnitude moves through the earth and uses the P-wave, an earthquake wave that travels through the earth and is the first wave that reaches the seismometer; while the surface wave or S-wave, travels along the earth's surface.

The Richter scale was replaced by the moment magnitude scale (MMS) because the Richter scale and other similar scales were not able to measure large earthquakes accurately. It was developed in 1979, by two Caltech seismologists Thomas Hanks and Hiroo Kanamori, to fix the limitations of the Richter scale and other measurement scales. The moment magnitude scale was more accurate for wide ranges of earthquake sizes and was able to be applied globally. This scale is based on the distance that a fault moved and the force required to move it. Moment magnitude is similar to the Richter scale for small to moderate quakes but it is more accurate for measuring magnitude 8 and larger quakes.

Earthquake Magnitude Scale

Magnitude	Earthquake Effects
2.5 or less	Minor, not felt
2.5 to 5.4	Light, minor damage
5.5 to 6.0	Moderate, slight damage
6.1 to 6.9	Strong, a lot of damage in high density areas
7.0 to 7.9	Major, serious damage
8.0 or greater	Great, can destroy areas close to epicenter

One more way to measure the strength of a quake is the Mercalli scale. This was invented by Guiseppe Mercalli in 1902 and uses the observations of witnesses to estimate the intensity of the quake. This scale is not scientifically accurate since witnesses may exaggerate the strength of the quake and witness testimony may not agree with each other. It also does not take into account the distance from the epicenter, the ground that the buildings are built on and the way the structures were designed.

Earthquakes release energy in seismic waves. A seismic wave is a burst of energy that is released during an earthquake or explosion within the earth; these are the energy that is measured by seismographs. Different types of waves shake the ground in different ways and travel at different velocities. There are two types of waves, the body waves and the surface waves; body waves travel through the earth and surface waves travel along the surface of the earth. There are two types of body waves the P wave and the S wave. The fastest wave is the P wave or the primary wave. This is also called a compressional wave, it is the first wave that you will feel during an earthquake, it pushes and pulls the rock as it moves. That first bang that you feel during an earthquake that initially rattles the windows is a P wave. The second body wave is the S wave or secondary wave, this wave moves slower than a P wave and can only move through solid rock unlike a P wave that can also move through liquid. This wave will shake the ground up and down and back and forth in the direction that it is traveling.

Surface waves travel along the surface of a quake and have a lower frequency than body waves. They are responsible for the damage that occurs during an earthquake. It is one of the reasons that an earthquake that is located deep underground will not do as much damage as a similar magnitude earthquake that is located closer to the surface. There are two types of surface waves a love wave and a Rayleigh wave. The Love wave which is named after A.E.H. Love, a British mathematician, is the fastest surface wave which moves the ground side to side, the motion is only horizontal. The second surface wave is the Rayleigh wave named after John William Strutt, Lord Rayleigh. The Rayleigh wave moves the ground up and down and side to side in the direction of the wave movement. This wave produces most of the shaking during an earthquake.

What You Can Do to Be Prepared

The best way to survive a disaster is to be prepared. Most disasters can happen at any time and you may be on your own for three days to a week before help can reach you. Learn about the disasters or emergencies that may occur in your area.

Find out how local authorities will notify you during a disaster and how you will get information, whether through local radio or TV, NOAA weather radio stations, or even text messages. You have all heard the test broadcasts from the emergency alert system (EAS); you may have even heard actual emergency information broadcast. This is a national warning system that requires all broadcasts to have a system in place that interrupts programming for the distribution of emergency information; this includes local broadcasters, cable systems, satellite radio and television. The FCC (federal communications commission), FEMA (federal emergency management agency), NOAA (national oceanic and atmospheric administration) can all use this system to communicate an emergency. FEMA is the only organization that can utilize this system nationally. When an emergency broadcast is transmitted, make sure that you listen to the information being given and listen to any instructions that pertain to you. You should also sign up for text message alerts so that you can receive warnings no matter where you are. These are called Wireless Emergency Alerts (WEA) and are sent by the government through your mobile carrier. Also sign up for your local emergency alert system, there is a link to the participating list for each state on the FEMA website. You can sign up on the FEMA website at https://www.fema.gov/integrated-public-alert-warning-system . The alerts that you will receive include extreme weather and weather emergencies, AMBER alerts and Presidential alerts for a nationwide emergency.

Know the difference between watches and warnings and what actions you should be taking for each kind of weather event. A weather watch means that there is potential for a severe weather condition to develop. For instance, a tornado watch means that the atmospheric conditions have not yet, but can form a severe thunderstorm that may develop into a tornado. No action needs to be taken for a watch, but you should be ready to take action if the watch is upgraded to a warning. A weather warning means that certain conditions have been met and severe events are developing or are imminent. Be aware of the warning areas and take any precautions that are necessary or follow instructions that the emergency alert system has given to you.

What can you and your family do to prepare for an emergency. It is a good idea for one member of your family to be trained in first aid and CPR. Encourage your friends and neighbors to be informed and to be prepared. You should have at least three days to a week worth of food and water per person, and that includes any pets. Be sure to create a disaster kit for your family and your pets. See the chapter of creating a disaster kit. I am sure that you remember the news footage after Hurricane Katrina; it took a long time for help to be mobilized and to get to the area. Many of the evacuees were staged in the Houston Astrodome where they had no food or water. Many of the residents chose to stay and ride out the hurricane, they had been through many before but no one knew how large this one was or that the levees would break. The people were not ready for the degree of devastation that the hurricane brought. The government did not have preparations in place for this kind of disaster and the residents were cut off from any kind of aid until help could be mobilized. In the event of a disaster you need to be prepared, it may be the only way that you and your family might make it through until help can arrive.

Disasters can happen at any time, so you should have a plan in case your family is not together. First you will want to have a safe place that you can meet, the first choice is right in front of your home, but this may not be possible in case there is an evacuation, so a second meeting place outside of your neighborhood would be a good second choice. In case of a more catastrophic disaster, where landmarks and buildings are destroyed, or you can't return to either meeting place, it is a good idea to have an emergency contact that lives out of state so that your family can coordinate a meeting place. Have an emergency contact card and keep it with you with the contact information for each family member (work, school, cell phones); print a contact card for each member of the family.

In case of an evacuation, decide where you would go and how you would get there. Practice the evacuation plan at least twice a year and try to plan alternate routes in case your initial route is not passable. If you have a pet, make sure your plan includes them; make sure that you have a list of pet friendly motels along your evacuation route. Make sure you do not let your gas tank get under a half a tank, preferably keep it close to full at all times, if an emergency happens you may not be able to get gas for quite a while. You can also register on the Red Cross, Safe and Well website to let your family and friends know that you are safe, or you can call 1-800-RED CROSS and select disaster.

Pets are members of the family too and you will need to prepare a disaster plan for them as well. You should keep a list of hotels/motels in the area that accept pets, and find out if they have any restrictions. Also keep a list of hotels/motels that accept pets in case you need to evacuate farther away from home. Another good resource would be veterinarians or boarding facilities on your evacuation route. You can also ask friends or relatives outside of your area if they could shelter your pets in case of emergency. You should also get a pet rescue sticker where you can list the number of pets that you have what kind of pets and your veterinarian's phone number, place this in a visible area like a front window or door so that rescue workers know what they are looking for. If you evacuate with your pets write EVACUATED over the sticker so no one wastes time looking for your pets.

It is a good idea to have earthquake insurance, especially if you are living in an area that is prone to earthquakes. Most insurance companies offer earthquake insurance and will be able to tailor a policy for your situation. You can find out more information by speaking to your insurance agent.

Earthquake Proof Your Home

One way to protect yourself and your family during an earthquake is to earthquake proof your home. During an earthquake your house will shake, most times it is very minor, but in the case of a large earthquake there may be a lot of damage in your home. You can minimize this damage by being prepared.

First and most important is the building itself, if there is a strong earthquake the building can actually shake itself off of its foundation. Once this happens, the house will collapse. You can ensure that this does not happen by having your home bolted to the foundation, or if your home is on pier and post foundations, make sure they are braced. If your foundation is brick or unreinforced masonry you should replace it with reinforced concrete. Brick or unreinforced masonry will collapse during severe shaking. The walls of the building are also prone to collapse if they are unreinforced and made of bricks, cinder blocks, clay tiles and adobe. A solution for this is to reinforce the walls with steel frames that will keep the walls from collapsing and possibly killing someone in the process.

The next thing you will want to do is to install a shut off valve on your gas line. During an earthquake the gas lines may rupture and cause a fire. The shut off valve should shut off the gas automatically during an earthquake, so you don't have to worry about a fire too.

You can also install flexible gas and water pipe fittings to appliances so they don't rupture as well. You should buy a bracing kit for your water heater to keep it from tipping over during an earthquake; this kit includes metal straps that are secured to studs in the walls. If you have a gas tank in the house secure it to the wall in a similar way to the water heater. Free standing fireplaces and woodstoves should be secured to the ground with metal brackets.

Furniture and other items can easily fall over during an earthquake; even a mild earthquake can cause some damage. One way to avoid this is to attach furniture to the walls to prevent them falling over, you can purchase furniture straps at any hardware store or use metal brackets that are secured to wall studs. Televisions and computers and other expensive equipment should also be attached to a secure surface, there are kits available to do this as well. You can also use picture hanging strips on smaller appliances to secure them in place. During shaking cabinets may fly open and the contents may fall out, there could be glass all over the floor. You should get child proof latches or earthquake specific latches for your cabinets; they allow the cabinets to open only a couple of inches until you unlatch them. This should prevent the contents from falling out. Anything with wheels should be secured so it can't roll around, an example is the refrigerator. Pictures that are not secured can easily fall off the walls during an earthquake. First, do not hang heavy pictures over the bed or the couch where they can fall and hurt someone. I prefer to use picture hanging tape to secure my pictures; they are flat against the wall so there is no shaking. Another option is a close hook, there are different sizes for different sizes and weights of pictures, attach a strong cord or wire to the picture frame and hook it onto the close hook and then click it closed. What about the books on the bookcase? You can run cord or wire across the front of the books to keep them from falling out during a quake. Don't forget your children's rooms; make sure their beds are not near the windows in case of falling glass and that there is nothing that can fall on your child during a quake.

We all have small items on our shelves. These will probably fall over and break during an earthquake; you can get something called quake putty or something similar at the hardware store to secure these items to the shelves. This is a clay-like substance that you roll into small balls and stick between your items and the shelf to hold it in place. It does not damage furniture and can be easily removed.

Building an Earthquake Kit

When a disaster strikes it usually comes without any warning. You must be prepared for any kind of disaster and the best way to do that is first to make a family disaster plan and then create a disaster kit. Make sure everyone in the family knows where the kit is stored and not to use items from the kit until an emergency strikes. Since a disaster can strike at any time, you should also keep a small kit in your car and at work in case you are not at home or able to get home. These are some of the items that you should keep in your disaster kit:

- Water- 1 gallon per person per day (3 days to a week's supply and don't forget pets)
- Food- 3 days to a week's supply, ready to eat or able to be prepared without cooking
- First Aid Kit
- Copies of Important documents and phone numbers
- Warm clothing and rain gear
- Heavy work gloves
- Bleach and an eyedropper or water purification tablets
- Women's hygiene supplies
- Hand Sanitizer, soap
- Plastic Sheeting or a Tarp

- Duct tape
- Utility Knife
- Blankets, Sleeping Bag
- Tent
- Heavy duty plastic garbage bags
- Medication
- Tools
- Flashlight
- Batteries
- Battery Operated or Crank Radio
- Whistle
- Dust Mask
- Pocket Knife
- Cash (Electricity may be out in a large area, which means ATM's will be down)
- Sturdy Shoes
- Local Map
- Photos of Family Members and Pets
- Toothbrush and Toothpaste
- Solar Charger
- Glow sticks
- Camp stove and Propane
- Toys to keep children entertained
- Insect Repellent
- Sunscreen
- Towels
- Matches or lighters
- Rope
- Candles and matches (waterproof)
- Toilet Paper

- Small fire extinguisher

How to make water drinkable

How to Make Water Drinkable Using Chlorine Bleach		
Amount of Water to be Treated	Treating Clear Water	Treating Cloudy, very cold or surface water
1quart/1 liter	2 drops	4 drops
1/2 gallon/2 quarts/2 liters	5 drops	10 drops
1 gallon	8 drops	16 drops
5 gallons	1/2 teaspoon	1 teaspoon
10 gallons	1 teaspoon	2 teaspoons
* Mix well and let stand for 30 minutes. The water should smell a little like bleach when it is done.		

Creating a Disaster Kit for your Pet

If you have pets, you should also create a disaster kit for your pets. These are the items recommended by the Red Cross:

- Medications and Medical Records (In a waterproof bag, like a Ziploc bag)
- Pet First Aid Kit
- Sturdy leashes, harnesses or carriers to transport your pet safely and so they can't run off
- Current photos, in case they get lost
- 3 Days to a weeks' worth of food and water

- Bowls
- Litter Pan and Litter
- Manual can opener
- Information on feeding schedules, medical conditions, behavioral problems and the contact information of your veterinarian
- Pet beds or toys

Building a First Aid Kit

It is important to have a well-stocked and up to date first aid kit. You never know what kind of situations that you may be in and having a well-stocked kit could save your life. You will want to store your supplies in an easy to carry, lightweight container, a tool box or fishing tackle box make good choices. The items listed below are a good basic kit for any emergency; you may want to add other items.

- First Aid book
- Scissors
- Tweezers
- Thermometer
- Pocket knife
- Needle and thread
- Tissues
- Cotton pads
- Heat packs
- Cold packs
- Splint materials
- Q Tips
- Gauze
- Gauze pads
- Adhesive tape
- Ace bandage
- Band Aids
- Butterfly closure strips

- Alcohol pads
- Hydrogen Peroxide
- Antibiotic ointment
- Aspirin
- Other pain relievers (Advil, Tylenol, Aleve)
- Diarrhea medicine
- Eye Drops
- Allergy medicine, antihistamine
- Aloe gel (for burns)
- Latex gloves
- Hydrocortisone crème
- Safety Pins
- Liquid bandage
- Eye pads
- Poison Ivy/Oak treatment
- An Epi Pen would be good if you can get one
- Rehydration Salts
- Vaseline
- Puppy Pads or Menstrual Pads (Good to soak up blood from wounds)

What to Do During an Earthquake

What should you do when an earthquake strikes? It really depends on where you are and the severity of the earthquake. For small to moderate earthquakes there is usually very little damage or injury, but for a large earthquake the steps that you take could save your life.

If you are outside, do not enter any buildings in case of falling objects of even the collapse of the structure. Stop where you are and look around, if something were to fall or a building were to collapse would you be in danger of being hit? If the answer is no, then stay where you are and wait until the earthquake is over. If the answer is yes then you need to assess the area and find the best place to wait out the earthquake with the least threat of damage or injury to yourself, an open area like a park would be a good place to wait. If you are in a mountainous area there may also be the threat of landslides, you will want to get into a safe area where the danger to you is minimized. Tsunami's can be triggered by large earthquakes; if you are in an area where there may be a tsunami threat, get to higher ground.

If you are in a vehicle you may not feel the earthquake at first, your car would absorb the vibrations. Once you realize that an earthquake is occurring you will need to assess your safety. If you are in an area where falling debris or building collapse is a possibility you will want to get to a safer area if that is possible. If the road is blocked and there is danger to you of falling debris you should get out of your car and get to a safe place, preferably an open area. If you are on the highway and you can pull over safely you should do so. There may be a danger of collapsing overpasses so make sure that you are not in the way of an overpass that may fall and if you are travelling on an overpass or an elevated roadway please try to exit off as soon as possible. Even after the earthquake has stopped try to avoid getting back on overpasses or elevated roadways until a structural engineer has declared them as safe.

Most people will be indoors when an earthquake strikes. When you feel an earthquake do not go outside or move around your house, you may be hit by falling debris. You should get under a solid object like a desk or a table and cover your head. You will be protected from falling objects by staying under a desk but that will not protect you from shattering glass which is why you need to cover your face and head. Wait until the shaking stops before you move and watch out for broken glass. This is a good time to get shoes on and grab your earthquake kit. Depending on the severity of the earthquake you may want to exit the building quickly before an aftershock hits, get outside into an open space where falling debris won't injure you. If the earthquake occurs overnight you will have to be exceptionally careful, being prepared with shoes near your bed could save you from an injury. The best thing to do is to stay in bed and cover your face with a pillow. Once the earthquake has stopped, grab your earthquake kit, shoes and a flashlight and depending on the damage you may want to get out of the house. If there is structural damage an aftershock could cause a collapse.

What if you are at work? The same steps should be taken as anyone indoors during a quake. You will want to get under your desk and cover your face and head. Most offices use fluorescent lighting and if an earthquake shakes them loose they shatter in all directions when they hit the ground. Office buildings tend to have a lot of windows, stay away from any windows and outside walls, the windows could shatter or debris could come through them. Do not use the elevator, a large quake could knock out the power and you would be trapped in there, or the quake could cause structural damage to the elevator and cause it to fall.

If you are in a public place, either indoors or outdoors do not panic. Look around you for a safe space and get to it, cover your head and face. Let me give you an indoor example and an outdoor example; you are at a baseball game in a crowded stadium, as you are enjoying the game a massive earthquake strikes. Do not panic and run into the building, there will be many people that do so and there is not only a danger of being struck by debris, but also of falling and being trampled by panicked fans. The best option is to stay where you are and crouch down and cover your head. Most stadiums in California are built to withstand large earthquakes so you should be fine. Public places like this have emergency exit plans to evacuate people safely. An indoor example would be a grocery store, imagine that you are doing your weekly shopping when a large earthquake strikes. Now a supermarket will have a lot of falling objects, so you will want to get out of the aisles and head towards the front or back of the store, then crouch down and cover your head; stay away from the windows. Once the quake has stopped, exit the store carefully since there may be broken glass.

What to Do After the Earthquake

The earthquake is over, now what do you do? The first thing is to check to see if anyone is injured. Provide medical aid for injured persons and if there are collapsed buildings see if anyone is trapped and requires help. Any severe injuries should be reported to local authorities, although depending on the scope of the damage they may not be able to get there to provide aid. If this is the situation, provide whatever aid you can and keep the person comfortable.

The next step should be to check your home for damages, especially to gas lines or to electrical wiring. If you smell gas, shut off the main gas line, someone from the gas company will need to come out and check your gas lines before turning it back on. If you notice damage to the wiring shut off your electrical box until you can have someone come and repair the damage. Check your foundation, walls and roof for damage or cracks, stay away from the chimney since they are weaker structures and may still fall over.

Clean up broken and fallen objects as long as your home is safe to do so. Be careful opening cabinets since the contents may have shifted and will fall when you open them.

It is a good idea to stay off the phone unless there is an emergency, phone lines may be down and cell towers may be damaged. You should have developed a family disaster plan and everyone should be following their role in where to meet. If the damage is really severe and landmarks are no longer visible each member of the family should know to contact the out of state emergency contact person to find out where to meet.

Even if the roads seem clear avoid driving if possible to keep the roads open for emergency vehicles.

If your home is severely damaged you can go to a shelter until you can repair the home. Text SHELTER and your zip code to 43362 (4FEMA). This information comes from the the FEMA website.

You will want to keep informed about what is going on and any instructions that are given by emergency services so watching TV or listening to the radio will be important. If you have no electricity you will want to use your battery or crank powered radio (one of the items that should be in your earthquake kit).

####

Links For More Information

http://earthquake.usgs.gov

http://www.ready.gov/earthquakes

http://www.fema.gov/earthquake

http://www.shakeout.org

http://emergency.cdc.gov/disasters/ earthquakes

http://www.redcross.org/prepare/di saster/earthquake

About Linda Bohm

Linda Bohm is a blogger, writer, jewelry designer and is fascinated by disasters. She has created a Disaster Preparedness website and blogs about disasters weekly. Linda enjoys watching disaster movies and researching disasters.

Other Titles by Linda Bohm
Rapture Survival Guide

Connect with Linda:
Website:
http://preparefordisaster.weebly.com
Facebook:
https://www.facebook.com/LBohmAuthor
My Blog:
https://devastationanddisaster.wordpress.com